If God is a Poet

Ron Barton

If God is a Poet

If God is a Poet
ISBN 978 1 74027 792 1
Copyright © text Ron Barton 2012
Cover image: Chloe Forster

First published 2012
Reprinted 2015

GINNINDERRA PRESS
PO Box 3461 Port Adelaide SA 5015
www.ginninderrapress.com.au

Contents

Speak Easy	7
Chalkie	9
Emotional Weaponry	11
The Thought Process of a Poet	12
Manly Men	13
Poetic Fallacy	14
A Yarn	16
Shits and Giggles	17
A Philanthropist's Notebook	19
A Sign of the Times	20
I Am the God You Seek	21
Cry of the Jungle King	22
Cry of the Jungle King: Part Deux	23
Conversations	24
You Are Not Yet You	25
Our Leafy Lives	27
Everything's Ash When It's Burnt	28
Fate Limerick	29
Religion Limerick	30
Aussie Ostracism	31
Superman	32
Verbal Masturbation	33
Advertising	34
Mousy-Mousy Poopy on the Shelf-Shelf…	35
Contagion	36
Aargh!	37
Seriously?	39
Adam	41
Signs	42
Again	43
Surface Paradise	44
Americarne	45

The Rhino and the Oxpecker	46
Life	47
Life's Loss	48
Boundaries of the Soul	49
The End	50
The Sin Cycle	51
Not Spandex	52
Purgatory	53
On a Wing and a Prayer	54
Alone in a Crowded Room	55
My Secret Crush	56
Lullaby	57
The Last Dance	58
Darkness on the Midnight Express	59
Daylight	60
Sleepless Sonnet	61
Street Scenario	62
Two-faced	63
Where I'm at	65
A Lesson	67
Ch!ld K!ller	68
Watered Down	69
Who am I?	70
Testosterone, Leather and Hops	71
The Teacher	73
The Self	74
Family	75
The Great Aussie Bush	76
A Contrast of Colour	77
Saturday at the Moon	78
How to Dissect a Poem	79
Paedophilia is the new Black	81
Seasons	82
If God is a Poet	83

Speak Easy

Chalkie

Oh, I'm sorry. Was it not clear enough? Did you not hear enough to know what to do? Where does the blame fall; is it on me or you?

'Cause I'm standing up here at the front of the class, busting my arse to get you to pass but, then, you don't do the work. And you might think I'm a jerk because I shout once in a while and I refuse to smile on the day an assignment's due. Well, that's bloody hard to do when I'm disappointed in what I get back because you're too slack to do it. You say 'screw it'.

But I've sat too many hours working at home; telling my wife and kid to leave me alone because I'm thinking of you and what you want to be.
Well, what about me? Can't you see things from my point of view?
This is not what I wanted to do.
I wanted to sculpt minds like an artist does with clay.
I chose this career to make a difference every day,
Not to babysit some little shit who'd rather spit on me than listen to what I say.

Yet, I wake every morn just after dawn;
Shower and dress for school,
Because I'm desperate to find that jewel,
That's inside each kid,
That pearl of wisdom that's hid deep down inside –
Trying to hide from the taunts of peers.
Because, it's all between our ears,
These fears that hurt out chest,

As we hide the best of us from the rest of us,
And as each day goes by,
All I can do is try,
Because I know,
That when these kids grow,
They'll look back and say,
'He made a difference that day.'

Emotional Weaponry

You try to break me with tears
because you are a woman and, as a man,
my defences are weakened by your emotional weaponry.

You only have two types of offence: emotional and sexual.

When you won me over it was a completely sexual affair.
There was no here or there about it.
Short skirts, low tops, make-up.
Hand holding, thigh caressing, kissing.
I fell into the web you wove and you trapped me there;
your venomous fang paralysing me.

Now, as I begin to work myself free,
tears fall from your cheeks like bombs from the sky.
Your once heaving bosom heaves again,
but this time in anguish and I am defenceless.

I raise my white flag,
as you knew I would,
and become your prisoner of war –
to have and to hold, till death do us part.

The Thought Process of a Poet

I could write a sonnet on it.
Yes, that would suffice.
Perhaps a ballad would be better
Or a free verse, just as nice.

But I don't want to have to conform to a specific form. Because, poetry being poetry, it can be anything I want it to be. For as a genre it is still mostly undefined – an expectation that lines, rhymed, don't meet the edge of the page but, like a tiger released from its cage, I just want to be free. Free to write whatever I want to write because the only one who can say whether it is wrong or right is me. Now, I might still choose to use some personification that's tied to the senses; or a metaphor that breaks through your defences because it hits you so hard in the heart that you could count to ten while you wait for it to start beating again. Or I might just write something rather plain and repeat it enough so it's tough to get out of your brain. But that's assuming I have something to say that's worthwhile, that's worth deliberating over the style in which I present it to the extent it seems as important as what's being said.

And what if it never gets read?

Manly Men

I do not cry.
Big boys don't cry.
Big boys are manipulated into thinking that
emotions are for the weak,
so they bury them
and each setback, break-up or disappointment
is another shake of the bottle
in the lead up to another explosion;
a violent explosion of masculinity.

So, I punch.
I punch and I kick.
I punch and I kick because I am a man
and it is socially acceptable for me to do so.

But now I am confused
as a generation of boys
pluck and wax and colour.
They accessorise
and pop their collar
as they strut the streets
in their fake tan.
They cry because
they are sensitive
and now this has become socially acceptable too.

But, are they manly?
And if they are,
then what am I?

Poetic Fallacy

I could be a poet
because I have low self-esteem
brought upon through years of
mental abuse and verbal assault.

I could be a poet
because I lack the confidence
to speak but have the
knowledge to write.

I can write religious limericks
where serious content
belies the nature of the form.
I can write sonnets
about testicles and regrets
in an effort to distance
them from the relationships
of their historical peers.

I can hypothesise
and hypnotise.
I can inspire desire.
I can transport you
to other worlds
where the pen is mightier
than the sword
and knights arm themselves
with liquid paper
but still cannot
defend their minds
from the resonance
of my reasoning.

Words glanced
by chance
leave imprints on the
brain like an eclipse
on the retina.

And I,
I can see eye-to-eye with I
and, while I don't always like what I see,
it is almost entirely me.

And I,
I could be a poet.

A Yarn

'Fuck me dead,' I says –
Mouth hanging open like I'm catchin' flies;
Cigarette's got a death grip on me bottom lip as it struggles to stay in place.
I barely notice, but me beer's frothin' over like a rabid dog.
I just can't stop starin' at this sheila that's just walked into the pub.
She's unbe-fucking-lievable lookin';
Hair as blonde as beach sand, lips as red as coral.
She's wearin' this strapless number and I can tell she's not from around here.
She walks up to the bar and I slides up next to her.
She says somethin' to the barkeep in her foreign tongue and I asks her if she has any Australian in her.
When she says no I asks her if she wants some but she doesn't get my drift.
So I tells her she's like a sheepdog roundin' up my heart but all she hears is 'dog' and all of a sudden she's offended.
She gives me a fair slap and then I end up wearin' her freshly-ordered drink.
'Fuck me dead,' I says.
And she says,
'No, not even then.'

Shits and Giggles

A Philanthropist's Notebook

15.00   The zombies gather outside of the gate.
        They trudge along slowly dragging their feet behind them.
        Audible through the fence are their monosyllabic grunts.

17.00   The larger zombies rise.
        It is a slow and stiff process.
        Many of them have huddled in the same position for close to eight hours.

18.00   The two groups merge and the feeding begins.
        As the sun sets, they flock like moths around rectangles of light.

Thus is documented the demise of humanity.

A Sign of the Times

Our modern world is full of gack,
you say it, warp it, play it back.
Wrong way on a one way track,
now go back to the start.

Modern girl with mystic eyes,
trades in lies and alibis,
and to me it's no surprise
that what she sells is art.

Now you'll find her there in toilet stalls,
writing love notes on the walls;
tales of tongues and salty balls –
she'll only break your heart.

I Am the God You Seek

I don't know and I don't care
what's the colour of your underwear.
Have a look and you will swear
that I'm the God you seek.

And in your struggled search for me
your concrete jungle rivalry
must dissolve for you to see
you're strong but you are weak.

Now you must change your troubled ways
before you reach your end of days.
Trust in what the bible says
the world is for the meek.

And people of all shape and size
will occupy my heaven skies,
then you'll come to realise
I am the God you seek.

Cry of the Jungle King

The Lion sits and ponders why
His pants don't fit, they're on too tight.
And so he readjusts his fly
While other creatures say goodnight.

As blacks replace the browns and greens
The Lion sucks his tummy in
And curses why he bought such jeans
With legs too tight and waist too thin.

'One last try,' he is heard to state
And finds himself a better grip.
He howls as pain reveals his fate,
He's caught himself within his zip.

So now you know why Lion's king;
Who else could stand such suffering?

Cry of the Jungle King: Part Deux

The Lion sits up in his bed;
He howls and lies back down again.
He starts to search within his head
For reasons for his immense pain.

Alas, it was a crime of passion
That brought him to this hospital.
A victim of designer fashion –
Jeans (too tight), the zip, his ball…

And so to tell him of his fate
A doctor enters dressed in teal.
'I'm afraid we had to amputate,'
He says and then becomes a meal.

The Lion sobs, how's he to strut
Through jungles now with just one nut?

Conversations

Female conversations are
epic novels
filled with rounded characters, glorious settings
and extensive back story.

Male conversations are
picture books;
Maximum meaning with minimal words.

You Are Not Yet You

'You are not yet you
so I tolerate your ways.
But you must grow up,'
he said, 'one of these days.'

'But, but,' I replied
though he'd heard it all before.
'It wasn't my fault.
I did, I tried to ignore

but they kept asking
and asking. I had no choice.
You'd know what I mean
if you had just heard his voice.'

'You are not yet you,'
he said. 'But it's a fool's way
to put too much stock
in what other people say.

Now remember this,
you're not vampire nor Pan
and one of these days,'
he cried, 'you'll be a man.'

'But,' I responded,
'I wasn't the only one.
Everyone else was…'
He cut in, 'Now listen here son,

you are not yet you
but that doesn't mean you can
let others decide
who you'll be when you're a man.'

'How long has it been,'
I cried, 'since you were my age?
You're so out of touch.'
My fists clenched in balls of rage.

'I am not yet me,'
I said, 'well that's nothing new.
But why should I listen
when you're no longer you?'

Our Leafy Lives

No skill or intellect have I
though joyful is the loving twig
that snaps as hands across it race
and feet of many dance a jig.

The life of laughter, lost and lonely,
bears but little similar
to that of mine or theirs or yours
whose lives are trapped within a jar.

The tree, of course, will carry us
through lakes and winding desert paths
that lead to windy mountain trails
and anywhere that we might ask.

And hiding are the little imps
and moles and trolls and pimples, three,
to lash out at our glassy home
and break the twigs from mother tree.

Everything's Ash When It's Burnt

The unforgiving, relentless torment
of life's demons piercing the buttocks of Man.

Blood flows like wine –
the water crescent
dives and dances
merrily upon the sea of faces.

Death's door opens
and welcomes the
solemn, sheepish
drones of the bordello.

The one hour scenic tour
departs daily
from the armpits
of hell
and Jesus
blasphemes as
he calculates the
effects of GST on alcohol.

The wallets lighten
and all signs
point towards
Slippery When Wet.

Look around:
what do you see?

Fate Limerick

Too many times I have found
That I'm only waiting around
For some sign
Of God's design
When fate, to action, is bound.

Religion Limerick

Once at a religious convention,
A man was asked not to mention,
That although he was there,
No belief and no care,
Had he for divine intervention.

Aussie Ostracism

To be an Australian
you must open your arms,
and our shores,
to all walks of life
from every corner of the globe
so that we have more people to mock
for being different.

To be an Australian
you must embrace our sporting culture
where football fields and cricket grounds
are hallowed turf
and we all dream of being sporting stars
while camped out on the couch
drinking beer.

To be an Australian
you must respect the role
that women have in our society
where even some ranga chick
can run the place.

To be an Australian
you must be in touch with the land
and have a love of the
great Aussie bush
while driving through city streets
in your suburban four-wheel drive.

To be an Australian
you must be a contradiction.

Superman

Please don't say that I'm your superman,
I can't do all those things you say I can.
I'm not the one on whom you should rely,
I am just an ordinary guy.

Life throws its weight around and we're all looking for a hero. While some might find solace in their peers or family, some look elsewhere. Ancient civilisations had their gods and warriors, modern societies have their war heroes and success stories, and children have their comic book heroes.

I'll be there when you really need me
But I'm not all you put me up to be.
I cannot allay all of your fears.
I also have to shed my own tears.

What we must consider, if we are to choose our heroes from those people around us, is the effect it has on their lives. While some people appear to be confident in their own existence, the extra pressure of being someone's confidant may be enough to upset their balance.

I can't fly, none of my powers are true.
I'm not super I'm just an also ran.
So if you get in trouble tonight
Your best chance for survival is you.
Please don't say that I'm your superman,
I just might be your kryptonite.

For all the advice we are offered, only some of it is ever as helpful as we hoped it would be. Sometimes the best course of action is to listen to your own heart and trust that you can be your own saviour.

Verbal Masturbation

The leader stands at the
front of the room
unleashing his verbal wank.

Specific jargon
designed to please
himself, not others,
spews from his mouth
over the unenlightened,
uninterested crowd.

To him,
policy documents are like porn magazines:
a string of vocabulary
built upon the premise
that the greater the syllable count,
the longer the orgasm.

All of it, however, is selfish as
we are all relegated to the role of voyeur:
There is nothing mutual
in this oratory orgy.

Advertising

In a world without advertising I wouldn't know
that sentient beings live inside my washing powder
lying in wait for unsuspecting stains
that prevent my sheets from being whiter than white.

In a world without advertising I wouldn't know
that smelling like a man, man,
and drinking the right alcoholic beverage
could lead to sexual encounters with super models.

In a world without advertising I wouldn't know
that having my athletic gear created by
Asian adolescents in cramped conditions
would increase my chances of becoming a sporting star.

In a world without advertising I wouldn't know
which politician to vote for
or which contentious issue
will result in me being taxed further.

In a world without advertising I wouldn't know
how beneficial a tiny portion of my pay cheque
might be to a child in a third world country –
or what toy comes in the latest Happy Meal.

In a world without advertising,
I just wouldn't know.

Mousy-Mousy Poopy on the Shelf-Shelf (aka Nature Versus Nurture)

On the fourth shelf behind the flour,
A mouse returns on every hour,
And feeds upon the golden stream,
Sweet and sticky like a dream.

And small round gifts he leaves for those
Whose syrup drips, and I suppose
That he's expressing gratitude.
Though some may think it rather rude

To relieve oneself upon a shelf.
Though you would do it, you yourself,
If toilet trained you never were
And your tiny body covered in fur.

Contagion

Language is contagious.

When my children were born
Neither of them could speak
But now, after extended exposure to their parents,
They have developed symptoms.
Grunts at first,
Vowel howls,
Then words.
My daughter, the oldest,
Is now forming sentences.
It appears as though they have caught English –
The most violent strain of language on the planet.
I fear it is too late for them now,
It may regress in their teenage years, as it appears to do in most.
I have witnessed this first hand,
in my classroom,
where I blacken my own soul
as an unwilling accomplice in the spread of this vile disease.
In the meantime, all I can do is pray for a cure.

Aargh!

My brain can't seem to process,
In a poem, my feelings of stress.
Try though I might,
I can't seem to write
What is making my thoughts such a mess.

Seriously?

Adam

The blackened eye of the woman who knows her place.
The blackened I of the man who told her,
hiding deficiencies and inadequacies
behind physical inequality.

The swollen cheek of the woman who stepped out of line.
The swollen pride of the man who corrected her,
feeling bigger than the boy
beaten by his father,
the boy whose
mother bled for him.

The broken jaw of the woman who questions her role.
The broken values of the man who scolds her,
trapped in an outdated, antiquated
way of looking at the world.

The beaten-down esteem of the man who is all alone.

Signs

There was a man on the street corner this morning.
He was looking down on me.
His red shirt stood in defiance of all I hold true and dear.
His defensive stance blocked all thought and feeling.
'This man knows me better than I do,' I thought to myself.
Later, when I was more calm,
I questioned whether I was reading too much into this interaction
When all he really said was, 'Don't walk.'

Again

It was a dark night.
The moon shone dimly behind the clouds.
Her naked body lay, cold, in the gutter.
Blood dripped across her sultry bosoms.
Her matted hair hid half of her face from the moonlight.
Her eyes, open wide, knew all:
the only eyes to witness her demise;
the way he ripped off her clothing;
the way he hit at her again and again and again;
the way he left her there.
Cold.
Dying, ever so slowly.
Besides him, she was the only one who knew.
In the final stages, her mind raced:
'The body will be found in the morning.
They'll search for him…
They won't find him…
They never find him…
They…'

Surface Paradise

The sun rises over the sandy shore.
Waves, playful in their movements,
tumble and fall as they run into each other.
The beach bronzed beauty queen,
toes kissed by the ebb,
giggles in giddy exuberance.
Her beautiful blonde locks,
bleached beyond repair,
hang over her buxom breasts
– surgically enhanced.
Her face,
on closer inspection,
made over and made-up,
presents a paradox to her physical pursuit.

This beauty is only skin deep and
this beach is where she belongs.

Americarne

The American vampires
fly through TV screens and radio speakers
to invade the western night sky.

Their sharp incisors
bite deep into language and culture
and drain out what was once
rich and lively, leaving only a husk.

Worse still,
the American vampires
fly over Middle-Eastern skies
swooping down over
insurgents and innocents alike,
stealing their life force.

Only time will tell
how far their wings
will spread.

The Rhino and the Oxpecker

The devil stood, larger than life.
On its back small creatures roamed.
They fed on its evil
and sucked its blood.

Then the angel came.

The winged saviour
brought salvation with a double-edged sword.
It clawed at the devil
and pecked at the helpless creatures on its back.

The irony is lost on them though;
That they fed upon the devil
just to become an angel's food.

Life

Time stops.
The inevitability of change dawns on you.
A reputation built over years is lost in a day.

Comfort.
Others remind you of how you helped them
And insist that you'll help others in your own special way.

Sorrow.
Those you've already helped are lost to you now
And as you move on, their memories will fade away.

Empty.
Life is endless torment.
You continue to mourn as you await the next day.

Life's Loss

Temptation:
Riddle me one more time –
I keep falling prey
to these questions in my mind.

Location:
Cardboard box – mobile home.
Hoping to find my way
now I'm all on my own.

Salvation:
Got my life on the line.
Hanging on day to day
but soon I'll run out of time.

Boundaries of the Soul

From out of the darkness came a beast more bat than man.
Leathery wings stretched out between its arms and its sides
like cobwebs in an attic corner.
Its face, grotesquely malformed, marred only by its perfect teeth.

Emerging from the light was an angel.
His soft, dove-like wings holding him aloft.
His face, an image of beauty, marred only by his bloodstained fangs.

In this ever-changing world in which we live,
the fine line between light and dark is often blurred.

Do you know your boundaries?

The End

The black churches bind,
the reign of God falls to the
armies of darkness.

Nature's mysteries
break the souls of man
and paint the streets with blood.
Humanity, however,
is the least humane –
sacrificing others to serve the self.

If we were made in the Lord's image,
then God is a masochist.

As the world crumbles
we must abandon our breeding
and revert to a pack mentality.

Only then can we truly live.

The Sin Cycle

The first sin,
born of wood,
grew into fruit,
and was taken by lovers
seduced by a serpent.

The first son,
born of God,
grew into man,
and was taken by Romans
afraid of the truth.

And so it was,
He died for all sinners,
from the fruit of the first,
on a cross made of wood.

Not Spandex

Where was Aquaman
when the dark, debris-filled depths
swept through Indonesian streets
drowning structures and cultures
as well as people?

Where was Captain Britain,
or Excalibur,
when bomb blasts
shook London to its core?

Where were the Fantastic Four
when the Twin Towers toppled
and America fell to its knees?
Where was Superman
when they retaliated?

Where were the heroes?
They were in the hearts and hands
of the survivors who toiled in the wreckage at ground zero.
They were in the minds and souls
of those who consoled the innocents
who lost loved ones.
They were there in their uniforms,
not spandex,
but badged and weighted with authority in their
red, white and blue.

Purgatory

I am but a shell of a man.
These once familiar streets I walk, crowded
with the souls of someone else's past.
In my heart
I know this is home.
Through my eyes
this is purgatory.
My soul, beaten into silence, feels nothing.
I am but a shell of a man.

On a Wing and a Prayer

The body of Icarus;
no longer visibly human.
Instead, it was a flat,
lifeless mess
of flesh, bones and blood
interspersed with shards of broken wood.
Snow-white feathers fell upon the pile,
chasing their over-zealous master.

When the body was finally removed,
an imprint remained embedded in the grass:

A blood-red angel.

Alone in a Crowded Room

Alone in a crowded room,
searching through the vast emptiness that is my heart and soul.

Tortured, punished by love and lust,
destined to walk this Earth alone.

A beautiful woman sits across from me;
her hair long and flowing,
her eyes deep and penetrating.

I know her type.
She is out of reach,
and I,
I am too young to die, too old to love again.

I am alone, in a crowded room.

My Secret Crush

Days have passed since I began my search
and still you elude me.
Many times I swore I saw you
but still you walk right through me.
Are you real
or just a figment of my imagination?
Only time will tell.
For now, I will continue my search for you;
my secret crush.

Lullaby

The meadow spring flows slowly by
as the lion sits and ponders why
he's cursed to live and never die:
This endless, mournful lullaby.

And angels floating in the sky
watch and listen as they fly
but seldom do they ever cry
for this lion and his lullaby.

As punished is he by God on-high
for living out a dreadful lie
and now under a watchful eye
forever lives in this lullaby.

The Last Dance

This is our last dance,
our last chance to say goodbye.
And though I leave with my head lowered,
I look back on our days together and smile.
But, now, as we step forward into the light,
I find that I can no longer stand the heat
and must return to the shadow.
As the music fades,
so too do I
blend further into the background
until all that's left
is the burning memory
of our last night together,
our last dance,
when I said
'Goodbye.'

Darkness on the Midnight Express

Darkness rides the midnight express
accompanied by the sounds of babies crying
and wolves howling at the moon.
Within the emptiness that is the carriage,
all manner of beasts converge upon
the recently deceased.
Forks of lightning split the sky.
Flashes of light fill the train.
Light. Dark. Light. Dark.
In a brief instant
the eyes can behold worse scenes
than ever imagined.
Sharp, blood covered fangs.
Mats of torn flesh and burnt hair.
Globules of mucous, blood and spit.
But the eyes need light to see
and in the horror,
Darkness is our only friend.

Daylight

The sun smiles down on the boy
who twists at the hips
with his head lowered,
fingers playing with his shirt.
The boy whose innocence
has not left him yet.
The boy who still dreams.

The sun beats down on the man
who bends at the knees
with his head lowered,
struggling to pick up the pieces of his life.
The man whose self-respect
left when his wife did.
The man whose dreams are now nightmares.

The son smiles up at the man
who raised him.
The son who doesn't know
why his mum is gone but
knows his parents still love him.
The man who cries when
he is alone and is
jealous of his son's strength.

Sleepless Sonnet

If only the sun would never rise
On days when you are not prepared.
For things that may cause your demise
Might not, but they still leave you scared.

And these things, you'll find, will not cease
And they're hard to trace back to the start.
The body cries out and begs for peace
To ease the pain upon the heart.

But in the silence and dark of night
The body rebels against the brain.
The need for rest, a reason to fight,
So the body's prepared to start again.

For there is a struggle in each new day
That rest alone will keep at bay.

Street Scenario

As I walk through the city where danger is life
I see the glimmer of a streetlight on a mugger's knife.
And in the shadows where he hides I see the glow of his fag
as he lifts it to his mouth for another drag.
I step left. I step right. I try to get around
but his fist is like a brick as he pounds me to the ground.
I struggle to my feet as he lunges with his blade
and my shirt is coloured red from the damage that he's made.
My mind becomes clear as I take my last breath:
Some loose change, a mobile phone; the price of death.

Two-faced

The seventeen-year-old
clings to her youth
like a little girl
to her mumma's leg.
She 'hangs' down
at the local park,
lounging on the
play equipment
with her friends
and eagerly awaits
the Royal Show
where she will soar
through the air
and gorge herself
on lollies and chocolate.

The same girl
embraces adulthood
like a long-lost lover.
She craves the ability
to buy booze
without a fake ID
and to drive,
not walk,
away from the
institutionalised hell
that is school.

The seventeen-year-old girl
is two faces
of the same coin
spinning endlessly –
asking of the future,
'Which side is up?'

Where I'm at

A Lesson

'T'was brillig and the slithy toves…'

What's a fucking brillig?

I said when we started that all you need to do is listen;
and that sort of language has no place here.

Now…

*'T'was brillig and the slithy toves
Did gyre and gimble in the wabe.'*

They're not real words.
You're making this shit up.

Just listen, please.
I am reading it
Exactly as it is on the page.

'All mimsy were…'

This is gay.

I can only assume you mean 'fun'
As inanimate objects cannot be homosexual.
Now, I apologise.
I chose this poem as it is one of my favourites
but perhaps I aimed too high.
Here's one that might be more appropriate…

'They fuck you up, your mum and dad.'

Ch!ld K!ller

Armed to the teeth I stand,
a sea of students before me.
Some chatter,
Some stand,
Others throw projectiles across the room.

I strike!
But no holy water
        nor silver bullet
                will work against these beasts.

Cornered, a light bulb springs from the top of my head...

I cage one like a canary.
In the mine that is society,
I hang Him.
His death, barely noticed,
        is mourned by few
                whose white masks muffle their warnings.

The End is broadcast on TV news,
missed by the comatose on the couch.

Watered Down

My personality,
        watered down like
                the pints of beer
        that pervaded my youth.

This, the price of fatherhood and responsibility.

Once a careless cavalier,
                I would spend nights
        making some mischief
or another.

Now I plant
myself on my daughter's floor
and pat and sing and stroke
until she sleeps.

Now I cradle
my son in my arms
and reinforce gender stereotypes
by calling him
'mate' and 'buddy'.

Now I go to bed
at nine-thirty
and spend my nights
sleeping and hoping
I'm not needed till the morn.

Who am I?

I am an explorer
of words;
blindly travelling through unknown lands
in a desperate attempt
to map the unconscious mind.

I am a detective;
searching for clues
to unravel the mystery
hidden beneath
layers of metaphors.

I am a surgeon;
slicing through symbols
and stereotypes
to reveal the
vital information.

I am an inventor;
creating elaborate meaning
from another's passion.

I am an English teacher.

Testosterone, Leather and Hops

Lace out passes of pinpoint accuracy;
Quick feet and quicker hands;
Celebrations, commiserations and chastising.

A bunch of blokes
on a field chasing,
not fame and fortune,
but the kind of collegiality and camaraderie
that's found in a bladder
contained within a leather pouch.

And afterwards,
the conversations flow in a
pace proportionate to that of the beer.
Late night, car-park conversations about
women
work
the umpires
women
family
women; and
sport.

And in the bond
that's formed these
boys become brothers.

And boys they are –
lads and larrikins
the lot of them,
when away from their
work and their wives.

But all games
come to an end
and the inaudible siren of
age and responsibility
is but moments from blaring,
so these lads live it up
while they can.

The Teacher

He sits and surveys his environment;
An empty classroom with messy desk and
messier floor. He takes some chalk in hand,
breathes in, and releases some of his pent

up anger on an unsuspecting door.
For every hour in which he looks
up teaching tools in scholar's books
he spends another hour, maybe more,

questioning why some students seem as though
they don't care about their education.
He was never short of motivation and drive,
whether teacher or parent stood as his foe.
But now, when asked of his vocation
he whispers, 'They have eaten me alive.'

The Self

Oft' I feel like Goliath
staring down at the boy and his slingshot,
refusing to believe that the boy is also me
as we all have the propensity
for tearing ourselves down.

Self-doubt and insecurity:
the rocks that lead to my downfall.
And in each victory
is the feeling of loss.

Oft' I feel like Icarus,
full of dreams and desire,
refusing to believe that my hubris
will lead to my downfall.

The harsh glow of the sun
melts away my pride
and exposes my insecurities
until I fall back to Earth.

Family

The phoenix sits atop my family tree.
History residing in its red breast;
Dictating what has come and what's to be.
All the while I am trapped within its nest.

My rebellious mother was far too
young and unprepared to raise her own son.
With little knowledge of what to do
I was left behind while she chased some fun.

My father, now dead, is the great unknown.
His ashes and secrets all that remain.
But what exactly are the seeds he has sewn?
This question, and others, coarse through my brain.

A parent now: the phoenix starts to burn.
My folks made their mistakes, now it's my turn.

The Great Aussie Bush

The wind blows through the branches of the banksias;
its unique smell – like a bouquet of dead ants –
fills your nostrils.
In the midst of the dense shrubbery
the red velvet of a kangaroo paw
catches your eye
and warms your heart.
Overhead, eucalypts stretch their hands
towards the sky.
Further down the beaten track
the blackboy stands
spear held high in the air,
protecting this pocket of perfection
from the suburban sprawl that surrounds it.

A Contrast of Colour

The setting sun brings black night
upon the red earth.

Long ago the people of this land
had their muddy water skin tainted
by the blood of their kin.

It was the white people
that spilt this blood
and, today, the red earth serves as a reminder
of the sins of our ancestors.

I am white,
but my soul has been blackened.

Saturday at the Moon

The creative collective are an eclectic bunch:
>The balding, the bawdy and the bizarre.

The suited child puts on a beard to better assimilate into the maturing crowd while the elderly couple reminisce about times forgotten.

The casual techie stares over his laptop screen at the microphoned maestro in the do-rag who captivates those who have gathered. His shirt flaps open like a rock god as he spews out words of wit, wisdom and winsome ways. His banter reaches a canter as he rants about politicians and loose women. At the end of his sermon he is greeted not with an 'Amen' but with applause.

How to Dissect a Poem

On your silver tray
a poem lies,
but before we can cut through
the surface we must
pin it down.

Transfer it to your
workspace,
cradling its delicate body
like a newborn baby.

Now, pin its upper limbs
down with your knowledge
of the author's context,
and the lower limbs
with your understanding
of the form.

With a steady hand,
make an incision in
the content to reveal its
inner glory.

Peel back the skin and,
alternating between scalpel and tweezers,
carefully remove all of
the internal organs:
similes, metaphors, personification,
alliteration, onomatopoeia.

The final step;
the most important.
Ensure you listen close…

Crawl into the space
you've made
and wear the
poem out to dinner.

Paedophilia is the new Black

The media moguls
publish pictures of prepubescent perfection
in low-cut leopard print
to the extent it seems
that this is the ideal.
Jour Apres Lunes –
'light of my life, fire of my loins'
– turns babes into babes
striking adult poses
in strappy tops.
The modern man –
'clutched my back behind your house
and sweated like a stallion'
– must question his conscience
in the face of a media barrage
that suggests paedophilia
is a fashion statement.
Understandable too
as everything old becomes new again;
there was no denial when Caesar met Cleo.
But, we are meant
to have evolved
beyond this
to see the ideal as an equal
in age and mentality.
Teenage girls may dream of Edward –
'I wrestled all night, while watching you sleep'
– but grown men should know better.

Seasons

We used to make love
but, alas, I fear that's all it was –
a love not earned or given freely
but made.
Made in the fiery pits of passion
that consumed our young, exuberant souls.

Now it is winter in our bed.
A cold wind blows through the valley
between our bodies.

Ice has formed on your heart
and your shoulders turned cold.
The drop in temperature
moves in to the rest of the house.

I find myself camped out on
the couch;
Blankets on, trying to maintain
the warmth,
waiting for the seasons to change.

If God is a Poet

If God is a poet
then I am a limerick,
crude and rude,
scribbled down in five minutes
after a night on the drink.
I am the man from Nantucket
whose sexual exploits are the stuff of legend
and, thus, imaginary.
Yet without these
I am nothing.
I have no substance
or meaning,
I simply exist
for the pleasure of others.
I am someone to laugh at,
to laugh with.
I am not the type of poem you read to your mum.
But you can read me to your older sister,
or a bunch of bawdy blokes
sharing beers and smokes.

Conversely,
my wife is a Shakespearean sonnet;
meticulously sculpted in iambic pentameter.
She could be compared to a summer's day,
though her eyes are nothing like the sun
they sparkle like the diamond in her engagement ring.
She makes my heart sing like Mary Poppins,

shrill yet delightful
and wrapped up in the warmth of childhood happiness and innocence.
She is the final piece to my puzzle,
the ... to my ...
and every other cliché from
every romantic comedy ever made.

www.ingramcontent.com/pod-product-compliance
Lightning Source LLC
Chambersburg PA
CBHW070050120526
44589CB00034B/1688